10/07

√

# Nature's Champions

## THE BIGGEST,
## THE FASTEST,
## THE BEST

# Nature's

# Champions

## THE BIGGEST, THE FASTEST, THE BEST

by Alvin and Virginia Silverstein

illustrated by Jean Zallinger

Random House 🏠 New York

*Library of Congress Cataloging in Publication Data*
Silverstein, Alvin.   Nature's champions.   Includes index.
SUMMARY: Discusses more than 25 plants and animals that have unusual distinctions
such as fastest runner, biggest eater, largest cactus, and oldest living thing.
1. Zoology—Miscellanea—Juvenile literature.   2. Botany—Miscellanea—Juvenile
literature.   [1. Animals—Miscellanea.   2. Plants—Miscellanea]   I. Silverstein,
Virginia B., joint author.   II. Zallinger, Jean Day.   III. Title.   QL49.S5168   574
79–20698   ISBN 0–394–84191–3   ISBN 0–394–94191–8 (lib. bdg.)

Manufactured in the United States of America     1 2 3 4 5 6 7 8 9 0

# Contents

*c. 1*

# The Fastest Runner

## THE CHEETAH

The cheetah is the fastest runner in the world. It has been clocked at up to 70 miles an hour—faster than the fastest racehorse. (The fastest a human has ever run is less than 28 miles an hour.) The cheetah is a sprinter, not a long-distance runner. In its home in the grasslands of Africa, its speed helps it to catch food. In the cooler parts of the day, in the early morning or just before sunset, the cheetah hunts. When it sees an antelope or gazelle, it slithers through the grass until it is less than 200 yards from its prey. Then it puts on an incredible burst of speed. Within two seconds, it goes from a standing start to a speed of 45 miles an hour. If the antelope or gazelle sees the cheetah in time, it dashes off, zigging and zagging frantically. If it can stay ahead of the cheetah for just 20 seconds or so, the spotted speedster will probably tire and give up the chase. But if the cheetah catches up with its prey, it knocks the fleeing animal over with its paw and quickly pounces on it.

Cheetahs are often called "hunting leopards." Both cheetahs and leopards are members of the cat family, and both have yellow fur with black spots. Both big cats hunt for food, but cheetahs can be tamed and trained to do their hunting for human masters as well. Carvings on Egyptian tombs several thousand years old show people taking the big cats on hunting expeditions. Marco Polo told of how Kublai Khan, the

Mongol conqueror of China, hunted with cheetahs in the thirteenth century. Tame cheetahs sat with their masters on horseback and then jumped to the ground when the game was sighted.

Some people have kept cheetahs as pets. But these cats can be dangerous playmates. Although they are as playful and affectionate as kittens (they even purr when they are petted), they may accidentally give a nasty scratch with their claws. The cheetah is an unusual cat. It is the only one that cannot pull in its claws.

Today cheetahs are in danger. They are fast disappearing from many parts of Africa and Asia. People have cleared so much land for farming that the cheetahs have fewer places to hunt. And in many areas the antelope and deer on which they feed have been wiped out. So many cheetahs starve to death. Hunters have killed thousands of cheetahs for their beautiful fur coats, or just for the sport of it. Scientists and nature lovers are trying to stop the slaughter of cheetahs and the other great cats. Unless they are successful, nature's champion runner may disappear from the world forever.

---

*70 miles = 112.6 kilometers*
*28 miles = 45.0 kilometers*
*45 miles = 72.4 kilometers*
*200 yards = 182.8 meters*

# The Largest Reptile

## THE SALT-WATER CROCODILE

Once, long ago, giant dinosaurs ruled the earth. The dinosaurs are gone now. Only some bones and fossil footprints remain to tell us that they once lived. But some of their relatives, the crocodiles and alligators, have survived. Scientists believe that they have changed very little over the last 70 million years.

The largest of all the living reptiles are the salt-water crocodiles. The biggest one ever measured was a huge man-eater killed in the Philippines in 1823. It measured 27 feet from the tip of its snout to the end of its tail. Its weight was estimated at a full two tons.

Crocodiles spend part of their time in water and part on land. They can lie in the water, mostly hidden, with only their nostrils and eyes showing above the surface. During the day, they often drag their long, scaly bodies up onto the bank to sun themselves. Basking in the sun warms their bodies. When they get too hot, they move into the shade or slide back into the water again.

When a crocodile is basking, it is peaceful and drowsy. Shore birds may hop about it without fear and even walk right into the crocodile's wide-open jaws to peck at the leeches clinging to its gums. But when a crocodile is hungry, it is a raging fury. It may knock its prey into the water with a swipe of its powerful tail, or grab it with a sideways snap of its huge jaws. The muscles that open a crocodile's jaw are very weak—so weak that a person could hold them shut with one hand. But the muscles that close its jaws are incredibly strong. French scientists found that a 120-pound crocodile could close its jaws with a force of 1,540 pounds. And a larger crocodile would be even stronger. Once the crocodile has its prey in the water, gripped in its powerful jaws, it pulls the victim under and drowns it. Then the crocodile rolls over and over until the prey is torn into chunks, which the crocodile gobbles down whole.

The terrifying stories of man-eating crocodiles are quite true. It is believed that salt-water crocodiles kill more than 2,000 people· each year in Asia, the East Indies, and Australia. The crocodiles of the Nile in Africa are also killers.

The female crocodile is a devoted mother. She builds a mound of earth as a nest for her eggs and stays close by to defend them for ten weeks or more, until they hatch. The baby crocodiles grunt when they are ready to hatch, and their mother digs them out. For a few days, they follow her around like baby ducklings. Then they scatter.

No one is sure how long a crocodile lives. But since they continue to grow slowly all their lives, it is believed that the biggest ones may be over 100 years old. In recent years, so many crocodiles have been hunted and killed for their skins that few have a chance to survive to great age. So large crocodiles have become very rare.

---

*27 feet = 8.2 meters*
*2 tons = 1.8 metric tons*
*120 pounds = 5.4 kilograms*
*1,540 pounds = 698.5 kilograms*

# The Largest Bird

## THE OSTRICH

What has two legs and is bigger than a basketball player? The ostrich, the world's largest living bird. It may stand eight feet tall and weigh as much as 300 pounds. It looks like a clumsy giant, but it is one of the swiftest runners in the animal kingdom. Running ostriches have been clocked at 50 miles an hour. Their two-toed feet are good for something else, too—kicking enemies. An ostrich's kick is so hard, it can break a lion's back!

The ostrich is a bird, but it can't fly. Its body is so heavy that its tiny wings could never lift it off the ground. And it does not have the right kind of feathers for flying. Ostrich feathers curl to form separate fluffy plumes. When an ostrich is sitting on its nest, it spreads its wings out like thick blankets to cover the eggs and keep them at just the right temperature.

Ostrich eggs are another reason for calling this bird one of nature's champions. They are the largest eggs laid by any bird—up to eight inches long and weighing as much as three pounds. You would need two dozen chicken eggs to make an omelet as large as you could make from just one ostrich egg.

In the 1700s, ostrich feathers were the height of fashion. Every well-dressed woman had to have a hat trimmed with ostrich plumes and an ostrich-feather fan. Hunters in Africa and Asia shot ostriches by the millions. Soon there were so few that it seemed they might disappear. But then it was found that the big birds could be raised on farms. Their feathers could be clipped off without even hurting the ostriches. In time the feathers grew back, and in less than a year they were ready for clipping again. Millions of ostriches were raised on farms in South Africa, Australia, and the United States. The best feathers sold for $500 a pound, and ostrich farmers made fortunes.

Then, suddenly, feathers went out of style. Ostrich farmers killed their birds or turned them loose. Soon they were scarce again. Now they are plentiful only in East Africa. There they roam with herds of zebras, gazelles, and other grazing animals. With their long necks and keen eyes, they act as "lookouts," warning other animals of danger.

Have you heard that an ostrich hides its head in the sand and thinks it is hiding from its enemies? The big bird is not as silly as that. What it really does when danger approaches is to lie down and stretch its neck out flat along the ground. From a distance its body looks like a bush or a lump of earth, and the enemy may not notice it.

---

*8 feet = 2.4 meters*
*300 pounds = 136.0 kilograms*
*50 miles = 80.5 kilometers*
*8 inches = 20.3 centimeters*
*3 pounds = 1.4 kilograms*

# The Most Shocking

## THE ELECTRIC EEL

All living things produce electricity. In most animals and plants, the pulses of electric current are so tiny that special instruments are needed to detect them. "Brain waves," for example, can be picked up by metal wires and disks called electrodes, pasted to a person's scalp. An electrocardiogram records the pulses of electricity from the heart. But some fishes are able to produce enormous amounts of electricity—enough to stun or even kill. The most powerful of these electric fishes is the electric eel. It can discharge up to 650 volts—enough to kill a person on contact. (The electric current we use in houses is usually only 120 volts.)

Electric eels live in the shallow, muddy waters of the Amazon and Orinoco rivers of South America. They are not related to other kinds of eels and resemble them only in their snakelike shape. The electric eel has no dorsal (back) or tail fins, as other fish do. It swims with the aid of a long anal fin, which runs nearly the whole length of the underside of its body. It can swim backward and forward, up and down, with equal ease. But most of the time it lives a lazy, sluggish life.

It does not have to work hard to protect itself and catch its food.

The electric eel is like a living storage battery. All of its normal body organs are crowded into the front fifth of its body. The remaining four-fifths is packed with more than 5,000 tiny electric generators.

The electric eel uses its electricity in several ways. When it swims, a small "battery" in its tail sends out weak electric pulses at a rate of 20 to 50 a second. The eel uses these electric pulses to find its way. They bounce off objects and come back to special pits in the eel's head. The eel uses electric "echoes" in much the same way that bats and whale sharks use sound to find their way around. (It is fortunate that the electric eel has this ability to navigate by electricity. As it grows older, its eyes are damaged by electricity, and it becomes blind. Actually, eyesight is not too useful anyway, in the dark and muddy waters in which the eel lives.) Scientists think that the electric eel may also use its weak electric pulses to communicate with other eels.

If an enemy threatens the electric eel, or a frog or some other possible prey is in the water nearby, the eel acts promptly. It turns on the powerful "main battery" that fills most of its body. Discharges lasting about 0.002 second are sent out in quick succession. An electric eel can continue discharging at a rate of up to 150 pulses a second without showing any signs of getting tired. Fishes and frogs are killed by the eel's strong electric shocks. A larger animal—even a horse that has come down to the water to drink—may be stunned and drown. But except for the gradual damage to its eyes, the eel does not seem to be affected by the electricity at all. In fact, other electric eels are often attracted to an area where one of their species is discharging. They flock to join in the feast.

The breeding of electric eels is still a mystery. During the rainy season of the year, they disappear from their usual homes. Perhaps they go to the flooded swamplands. When they return, small baby eels are swimming along with them. The young electric eels produce very little electricity. The larger they grow, the more powerful their electric shocks become. A full-grown electric eel is one creature you want to stay away from!

_____

*1 inch = 2.5 centimeters*
*5 or 6 inches = 12.7 or 15.2 centimeters*

# The Fastest Animal

## THE SPINE-TAILED SWIFT

Nature's champion speedster has only two legs and cannot run at all. Indeed, its short legs are so weak that it can hardly walk and rarely lands on the ground if it can help it. But it more than makes up for its weak legs with a pair of large, flat wings, powered by strong flight muscles. Most experts believe that the fastest living creature is a bird, the spine-tailed swift. The fastest flight that has ever been clocked took place in the USSR. There, a spine-tailed swift was seen flying at over 106 miles an hour.

The fastest of the spine-tailed swifts live in Asia. But there are other species living over much of the world, and some of them are also extremely fast fliers. The spine-tails that live in Brazil often dive straight down like missiles into the jungle ravines. Brazilians call these swifts

"rockets." The spine-tailed swifts that breed in the eastern United States are called chimney swifts because they build their nests inside chimneys. Like most of the other spine-tails, these swifts used to nest inside hollow trees. But when settlers moved in and built cabins and houses, the swifts found the man-made hollows more convenient.

Spine-tailed swifts do their courtings in flight and mate high up in the air. Then the pair go looking for a good nesting place in a hollow tree or a large chimney. Off they fly to get building materials. They tear off dead twigs from tree branches without missing a wingbeat and carry them back in their bills to the nest. Each twig is carefully cemented into place with a bit of saliva from the bird's mouth. Within minutes after the saliva has been exposed to the air, it becomes hard and firm. Gradually a bowl-shaped nest is built, glued to the wall of the hollow. Before the nest is even finished, the female swift lays several longish white eggs. She and her mate take turns sitting on the eggs for nearly three weeks. Then both work to feed and care for the young chicks.

After two weeks or so, the young swifts are out of the nest, exploring the hollow. Like their parents, they cling to the wall with their sharp claws. When their feathers have grown out, they use their spine-shaped tail feathers as a prop to help support them. After about a month, they take their first flights out of the nest.

The speed of the spine-tailed swift helps it to catch meals. It snaps up insects as they fly, high up in the air. Often the swifts feed at such great heights that people on the ground can't even see them.

_____

*106 miles = 170.5 kilometers*

# The Slowest Animal

## THE SNAIL

When something is happening very slowly, we sometimes say it is going "at a snail's pace." How fast does a snail go? It takes a lot of patience to find out. Snail watchers have found that garden snails at their speediest can cover as much as 55 yards in an hour, or about 0.03 mile per hour. But some snails creep along at less than two feet an hour—0.00036 mile per hour! The tortoise, another noted slowpoke, is a real speedster in comparison—when it's hungry, it can cover 5 yards in a minute (0.17 mile per hour). In snail races, a good winning time is 2 feet in 3 minutes. (The best human racers can run a **mile** in less than 4 minutes. A racing snail would take five and a half days to cover a mile.)

Of course, a race between a snail and a human would not only be silly, but unfair. The snail has only one foot, which is also the bottom of its body. (Snails belong to a group of animals called *gastropods*, which means "belly-foot.") A land snail moves by contracting the muscles in the sole of its foot, one after another, in a rippling wave that moves forward along the foot. The animal glides along smoothly on a carpet of wet, slippery slime that it dribbles out from an opening just under its mouth. After the snail has passed, shiny trails of slime mark its path.

A moving snail also has a heavy load to carry—you would move slowly too, if you had to carry your house on your back! The snail's soft body is covered by a hard, coiled shell. When danger threatens—perhaps a rat, a duck, a blackbird, or a human being—the snail can pull all of its body into the shell, so that the sole of its foot neatly plugs the opening. It also retreats into its shell in the hot, dry summers and in the cold winters, sealing the edges of the opening with slime. Snails can stay inactive this way, without eating or moving, for months or even years.

A snail is a funny sight as it comes out of its shell. First the "belly-foot" comes out. Then, at the front end of this soft belly-foot, two pairs of tentacles begin to poke out, as if someone were pushing out the fingers of a glove that was inside-out. When they are all the way out, the tentacles look like horns on the top and front of the snail's head. At the tip of each of the two larger tentacles is an eye. Imagine having your eyes up on stilts! The snail can look around by moving its tentacles, without having to turn its head.

Garden snails eat mainly leaves and fruit. They saw off pieces of food with a long tongue called a radula. A snail has teeth on its tongue—15,000 of them!—and it uses its tongue like a file. Garden snails can find their way back to their favorite feeding places, even if a gardener has thrown them away over a wall. They may be slow, but they get there.

As a snail grows, its shell grows, too (otherwise its body would get too big to fit into its shell). The only place the shell can grow is around the opening. The snail needs calcium minerals to build its shell. It gets them by cutting holes in lime-stone rocks with its file-like tongue and eating the powdery minerals it scrapes off. When the snail gets plenty of food and water, and the minerals it needs, it can add an inch to its shell in just two weeks.

It takes two snails to produce baby snails, just as it takes two parents to produce a human baby. But unlike people, snails don't come in males and females—each snail is both a male **and** a female. After two snails have mated, each one becomes a mother, laying from 40 to 100 tiny white eggs in a cluster in the soil. A few weeks later, the baby snails hatch. Each new slowpoke is only ⅙ inch long, but it already has a tiny, perfect shell of its own.

---

*55 yards = 50.3 meters*
*0.03 mile = 0.05 kilometer*
*2 feet = 61.0 centimeters*
*0.00036 mile = 0.00058 kilometer*
*5 yards = 4.6 meters*
*0.17 mile = 0.27 kilometer*
*1 mile = 1.6 kilometer*
*1 inch = 2.54 centimeters*
*⅙ inch = 4.2 millimeters*

# The Largest Living Thing
## THE GIANT SEQUOIA

The legends of many lands tell of giants who once walked the earth. A race of giants still lives on earth, but these giants do not walk. They are trees, firmly rooted to the ground. These are the giant sequoias of California.

The champion of all the giant sequoias is the General Sherman Tree. It measures more than 100 feet around its base and is over 270 feet tall. Its largest branch is 7 feet thick—a tall man could lie across it without even his toes hanging over. The General Sherman Tree is believed to weigh about 6,000 tons.

Many other giant sequoias are nearly as large as the General Sherman Tree. The giant sequoias are not the tallest trees in the world. Their relatives, the redwoods, can grow to more than 350 feet. But they're not as wide as a sequoia. Some baobabs and some Mexican swamp-cypruses have trunks that are larger at the base. But those trees don't grow as tall as the sequoias. So in sheer mass, giant sequoias are truly the biggest living things in the world.

Of course, the giant sequoia does not start its life as a giant. It begins on a pine cone as a tiny seed only ¼ inch long. The cones may cling to the branches of the parent tree for as long as 20 years. But at last they fall, and new seedlings sprout from the seeds. A young giant sequoia looks like a Christmas tree. It has a cone shape, with branches reaching down to the ground. As it grows, its lower branches fall off, and its bark thickens. The bark of an old giant sequoia may be as much as two feet thick!

The roots of the giant sequoias are surprisingly shallow. Most of them reach less than eight feet down into the ground. But they spread out over an area of as much as three acres (about as big as four football fields), so the trees are in no danger of blowing over.

Giant sequoias are unusually strong, healthy trees. Their thick bark protects them from insects; and if they get burned, they can grow new wood over the scars. Many of them are 3,000 to 4,000 years old, and they still produce new crops of seeds. Not one giant sequoia has ever been known to die from old age or disease.

A giant sequoia is a lumberman's dream. Just one tree could provide enough board feet to build 80 five-room houses. But so many have been cut down that only a small number of giant sequoias are left. Once they covered most of the land north of the equator. Now they are found in fewer than 50 groves, on the western slopes of the Sierra Nevada mountains. Groups of people are fighting to save the last of the giant sequoias.

*100 feet = 30.5 meters*
*270 feet = 82.2 meters*
*7 feet = 2.1 meters*
*6,000 tons = 5,400 metric tons*
*350 feet = 106.6 meters*
*¼ inch = 6.3 millimeters*
*2 feet = 61.0 centimeters*
*8 feet = 2.4 meters*
*3 acres = 1.2 hectares*

# The Highest Flier
## THE ALPINE CHOUGH

In 1953 a team of British mountain climbers climbed up to the top of Mount Everest, the world's highest mountain. Biting winds whistled past the climbers as they struggled up the peak. High up on the mountain a flock of black birds began to follow them. The air was so thin that the mountain climbers had to use oxygen masks. But the birds swooped and darted, soaring in the air and diving down to snatch up bits of food from the climbers' camp. The birds followed the climbing team all the way up to 26,902 feet—more than five miles above sea level! These birds were Alpine choughs, nature's champion high fliers.

The name of these birds is pronounced "chuff." But originally *chough* was pronounced "chow," after the sound of the birds' cry. Alpine choughs belong to the crow family, and they look very much like crows. But their shrill cries are much more musical than the harsh "caw" of a crow.

Alpine choughs make their home high up in the Alps and other mountains of Europe and Asia. They build their nests of twigs and mountain plants in cracks and in the rocks. Often the nests are lined with wool from the sheep that graze in the high mountain pastures. Choughs live on insects and grubs that they dig up from the soil. Sometimes they steal fruits and berries from gardens.

Mountain travelers find these champion fliers a thrill to watch. They seem to play in the air. Sometimes they ride the winds, soaring lazily upward. Then they may suddenly tumble and twist, turning somersaults in the air. Or they may just fold their wings and zoom straight downward. It seems that they will surely crash—but just in time, they level out. Few people ever get to see Alpine choughs at home in their nests in the high peaks. But many visitors to mountain resorts have a chance to watch these master fliers when they fly down and give their air show. Alpine choughs often become quite tame. They will even swoop down to snatch tidbits from tourists' hands.

---

*26,902 feet = 8,199.7 meters*
*5 miles = 8.0 kilometers*

# The Tallest Animal

## THE GIRAFFE

Two basketball players, one standing on the other's shoulders, could not match the height of nature's champion, the giraffe. The tallest giraffe that was ever measured stood 19 feet from the bottom of its hoofs to the tips of its horns.

A giraffe's legs are so long that a man could stand upright between them. Its neck may be longer than 6 feet—the height of a man. (Yet the giraffe has only seven neck bones, or vertebrae, exactly the same number as in the much shorter neck of a human being.) With those long legs and neck, taking a drink of water is a balancing act, and getting up after lying down would be a real problem. So giraffes normally don't lie down all the way. To rest, the giraffe folds its legs up underneath its body and crouches on them, and it lays its neck down along its back to sleep. Getting up takes a long time. The giraffe has to swing its neck first back and then forward, to take the weight off its legs as it unfolds them bit by bit.

The giraffe's height gives it an advantage over the other animals in the dry plains of Africa where it lives. Not only can it nibble on leaves from trees that other animals cannot reach, but it is like a living watchtower. Looking out over the plains with its keen eyes, the giraffe can know in advance if an enemy is approaching.

Giraffes are normally quiet, peaceful creatures. Their spotted coats help to camouflage them among the leafy branches of the acacia trees. If danger approaches—stalking lions or human hunters—they may take off in a fast, rocking gallop. Their long necks seesaw back and forth, helping them to balance.

One lion by itself would be very foolish to attack a full-grown giraffe. Kicks from the giraffe's heavy hoofs can kill, and it can butt with its head like a battering ram. Sometimes male giraffes fight duels, striking smashing blows with their heads. Their horns, rounded and padded at the tips, are not very good weapons. But a giraffe's head weighs 100 pounds. A well-aimed blow with it could break another giraffe's neck.

Giraffes do not use their teeth to bite leaves from the trees. Instead, they pull the leaves off with a long, strong tongue. They gulp their food down whole. Later they bring it up, a little at a time, and chew their cud like a cow.

Many people think that giraffes cannot make a sound. But they have large voice boxes, and sometimes they have been heard mooing or grunting softly. Young giraffes bleat like calves. Some scientists think that giraffes may communicate with ultrasound—sounds that human ears cannot hear.

A newborn giraffe is already as tall as a full-grown man, and it grows quickly on its mother's rich milk. The adults in the herd watch over the playful young giraffes. In six or eight years, the young giraffes are ready to have families of their own, and they may live for more than twenty years.

---

*19 feet = 5.8 meters*
*6 feet = 1.8 meters*
*100 pounds = 45.4 kilograms*

# The Keenest Hearing

## THE VAMPIRE BAT

"Blind as a bat" is a common expression. Actually, bats aren't blind, although their eyesight is rather poor. Living in dark caves and hunting at night, bats don't really need good eyes. They use another sense to find their way around: their sense of hearing. Bats have the keenest ears of all land animals. Among the bats, the champions in hearing are the vampire bats. Vampire bats can hear very high-pitched sounds, so high that humans could not hear them at all. In fact, these bats can hear sounds up to 150,000 cycles per second, more than seven times as high as the highest sounds people can hear.

What makes such high-pitched sounds? The bats themselves do. As a bat flies, it constantly sends out very high-pitched sounds. (The squeaks that people hear are only the lowest-pitched part of the bat's cries.) The sound waves bounce off objects and echo back toward the bat. The bat's large, pointed ears are like sound funnels. They collect the sounds and send messages to the bat's brain. The bat's brain is like a tiny computer. It takes all the sound messages and puts them together to form a picture of the world outside. This echo-location works so well that a blindfolded bat can fly through a maze of dangling wires. If the bat's ears were stopped up instead, it would bump into one wire after another.

Some bats use their high-pitched voices and sensitive ears to catch moths and other flying insects. But vampire bats have a different way of life. Like the vampires in horror stories, these bats live by drinking the blood of animals.

Echo-location helps the vampire bat find its prey—a sleeping animal

28

or human. Dogs can hear some of the bat's cries and usually are safe from bat bites. But cattle and people can't hear the cries and so have no warning. When the vampire bat locates its prey, it flutters in front of the unlucky animal. Something—either the vibrations of the bat's wings or perhaps a scent that the bat produces—seems to have a soothing effect on the victim. Usually he is not even aware that he is being bitten. The vampire bat may bite while it is flying, slashing with its razor-sharp front teeth. Or it may land on the ground or a branch nearby, run over to its victim on all fours, and jump on, then bite. The vampires of horror stories suck their victim's blood. But the vampire bat actually laps up the blood, rather than sucking it up. A chemical in its saliva prevents blood from clotting and thus keeps it flowing freely even from a small wound. Sometimes bats stuff themselves with so much blood that they look like little furry balls.

Losing blood to a vampire is a frightening thought, even when the vampire is a little bat just three inches long. Bites from vampire bats can be deadly. The bats don't drink enough blood to kill a person, but they may carry rabies and other dangerous diseases. People in Latin America, where vampire bats live, have good reason to fear these furry fliers.

# The Most Legs

## THE MILLIPEDE

The millipede does not really live up to its name. Though millipede means "thousand-legged," few millipedes have more than 200 legs. (The largest number of legs that has ever been recorded for a millipede is 355 pairs, or 710 legs.) But even 200 legs make the millipedes by far nature's champions. Centipedes, which generally have about 30 legs, are not even close.

A millipede's body is like a long tube made up of a series of jointed segments or parts. Usually two pairs of legs are attached to each segment.

With hundreds of legs, how does a millipede know which one to step with next? It does so naturally, without "thinking" about it, moving each pair of legs in turn down the length of its body. The flowing waves of movement make the millipede seem to glide smoothly along.

Most millipedes are vegetarians. They live on rotting plant matter and molds. They burrow through the soil, pushing their way into it or using their flat, wedge-shaped heads to cut their way through like a knife.

Birds, mice, and various insects prey on millipedes. But the millipede has a number of defenses. It may slip quickly into a crack in the soil or under a rock. Or it can use a kind of chemical warfare: two rows of "stink glands" along the sides of the millipede's body can give off a foul-smelling substance that contains the deadly poison cyanide. The amounts of this poison are so small that it would not harm a human, or even a mouse. Some millipedes play dead when they are attacked. Others curl up like a watch spring, with the

hard outer covering on their backs turned outward like a protective suit of armor.

Millipedes have a rather complicated way of mating. In some species, the male spins a web on the ground and places his sperm there for the female to pick up. He may lay down long, straight "roads" of a sticky material to guide the female to the web. Other male millipedes use special pairs of legs to give "packets" of sperm to the females.

After mating, one common type of female millipede builds a dome-shaped nest of earth and saliva. She lays her eggs through a hole in the top of the dome and seals up the nest. Then she curls her body around the nest and stays there, protecting her eggs until they hatch.

A millipede does not begin life with hundreds of legs. The babies that hatch from the eggs have only three pairs. But as they grow, they add segments, a few at a time. They continue to grow and add segments through their whole lives, getting longer and longer, with more and more legs.

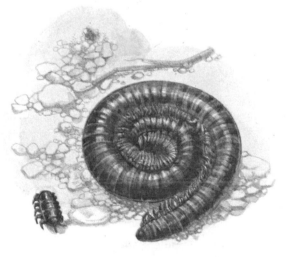

# The Largest Land Animal

## THE AFRICAN BUSH ELEPHANT

It would take more than a hundred men to equal the weight of just one African bush elephant. It is the biggest of all the living land animals. The largest one ever measured accurately was more than 33 feet from the tip of his trunk to the end of his tail. He stood about 12½ feet high at the shoulders. His weight was estimated at 24,000 pounds.

A giant-sized appetite goes with that big body. An African elephant eats tree leaves, grass, small branches, bark, fruits and berries, and other vegetable foods—up to 500 or 600 pounds of food a day. If it cannot reach the tender leaves at the top of the trees, it simply butts its head against a tree trunk until the tree comes crashing down. Or the elephant wraps its trunk around the tree and pulls it up by the roots.

Everything about an African elephant is big. Its baggy skin is an inch thick and may weigh a full ton. (Elephants belong to a group of animals called *pachyderms*, which means "thick skin.") Elephants bathe in water as often as they can to keep their skin in good condition.

An elephant's trunk is probably the most sensitive nose in the whole kingdom. It can sniff the wind and detect the scent of a human several miles away. The trunk is like a sensitive hand, that can feel the shapes and textures and temperatures of objects, pick up an item as small as a sugar cube, and caress the elephant's mate and young. It is also a mighty arm that can coil around a tree trunk, rip it out of the ground, and carry it like a matchstick. An elephant uses its trunk to carry food and water to its mouth, and it gives itself a shower bath with water squirted from its trunk.

Elephants have the largest teeth in the animal world. Their tusks are actually long incisors (front teeth). An African elephant's tusks can grow to more than 11 feet long and weigh well over 200 pounds each. These tusks are dangerous weapons in a fight. The elephant also uses them to dig up roots and even to dig for water in the dry season. Usually one tusk is larger than the other, for the elephant uses one side more than the other and that tusk tends to get worn down. An elephant also has four molars (grinding teeth), one in each side of each jaw. Each molar is a foot long and weighs eight or nine pounds. As it gets worn down from chewing, another molar pops out of the gum behind it. The new molar moves into place when the worn tooth falls out. An elephant can

replace its back teeth in this way six times.

A baby elephant takes about 22 months to develop inside its mother's body. No other animal takes that long to be born. A newborn elephant is a bouncing baby indeed—about three feet tall and 200 pounds. Just like a person, it takes about 20 years to reach its full size. Some people think that elephants live for hundreds of years, but actually their lifetime is about 70 years—just like ours.

---

33 feet = 10.0 meters
12½ feet = 3.8 meters
24,000 pounds = 10,886
   kilograms
500 or 600 pounds =
   226.8 or 272.2 kilograms
1 inch = 2.54 centimeters
1 ton = 0.9 metric ton

11 feet = 3.3 meters
200 pounds = 90.7 kilograms
1 foot = 30.4 centimeters
8 or 9 pounds = 3.6 or 4.1 kilograms
3 feet = 91.4 centimeters

# The Longest Migration

## THE ARCTIC TERN

An airplane can whisk a person halfway around the world in a matter of hours. But long before airplanes were invented, nature had its own world travelers—the migratory birds. These feathered fliers follow the changing seasons, enjoying warmth and good feeding all year round. It is amazing how they can find their way around without maps or compasses to guide them. As winter approaches, the birds leave their nesting grounds up north. Fleeing from the cold weather, they fly hundreds or even thousands of miles to feeding grounds down in the warm south. Then, the following spring, when the northern lands are warming up again, they fly back to the same nests they had before. Of the many migratory birds, the champion long-distance fliers are the arctic terns.

The long migrations of the arctic terns take them practically from the North Pole to the South Pole and back again. One tern was caught in northern Russia in July 1955, and a band marked with the place and date was put around its leg. The following May, the same bird was captured in Australia, 14,000 miles away. Other tern migrations of more than 10,000 miles have been observed.

The arctic tern's long journey begins in the far north, in the nesting colonies on tiny rocky islands. The nests are crowded together, each just far enough from the next nest to avoid being pecked at by the terns who live there. The tern's nest is not very fancy—a scrape in the sand, surrounded by a few pebbles and weeds. The arctic tern is a traveler, and it does not spend much time and energy on building.

Arctic terns mate and lay eggs during the long arctic summer, when the sun does not set for nearly four months. The spotted eggs hatch into clumsy chicks. The parents fly back and forth again and again between the water and the rocks, bringing fish for their hungry chicks. They defend both eggs and chicks from enemies such as rats, cats, owls, gulls, and humans. If the babies are threatened, the parents make a nose-dive and strike the enemy with their beaks.

When the young terns are a few months old, it is time to start the long flight to the southern feeding grounds. Depending on where the nest is located, their path passes over the Atlantic or Pacific Ocean. The birds spend many weeks in flight. Their route is not something they are taught—in some mysterious way, they know it as soon as they are old enough to make the first flight. A young bird can guide itself to its ancestors' feeding grounds even if it becomes separated from the flock.

Down in the Antarctic, near the South Pole, after the long flight, summer comes again for the arctic terns. (It is winter in the northern lands that they left.) They will enjoy another four months of continuous sunshine before they must start on the long flight up to the north to meet the spring again.

*14,000 miles = 22,526 kilometers*
*10,000 miles = 16,090 kilometers*

# Layer of the Most Eggs

## THE OCEAN SUNFISH

The ocean sunfish is a peculiar-looking creature. It looks as though someone had sliced off its back half, just behind its head. (Indeed, some people call it a "headfish.") Its tail fin is scarcely there at all—just a fringe at the end of its body.

The ocean sunfish is the heaviest of all the bony fishes. Full grown, it may measure up to 10 or 11 feet long and weigh a ton or more. The heaviest ocean sunfish ever measured was caught accidentally when it got stuck in a ship's propeller. It was 10 feet long and 14 feet high, and it weighed 2¼ tons. Imagine catching **that** on your fishing line!

The ocean sunfish is not only a champion heavyweight among the bony fishes, it is also a champion in another way: it lays more eggs than any other living creature. The body of one female was found to contain 300 **million** eggs.

Considering the size of the mother sunfish, her eggs are amazingly tiny—only about ¹⁄₂₀ inch across. The tiny fish that hatches from the egg is about ¹⁄₁₀ inch long. Compared with its mother, it is like one rowboat next to a fleet of 60 ocean liners.

Just-hatched ocean sunfish do not look at all like their parents. They have a normal fish shape, and soon they become covered with a coat of spines. Gradually the spines are lost, and the body starts to take on a flat shape. By the time the young fish is ½ inch long, it is beginning to look like a tiny copy of its parents.

As the ocean sunfish grows, it begins to spend much of its time on its side, floating lazily in the surface waters. It feeds on jellyfish and tiny ocean creatures. It swims with its dorsal (back) and anal (belly) fins, which sometimes flap out of the water. And it uses its tail to help keep its balance. The ocean sunfish steers by squirting jets of water out of its gills or from its mouth.

Young ocean sunfish may be gobbled down by other fish. But once they have grown large, they have few real enemies. The adult ocean sunfish has a tough, leathery skin, backed by a layer of rubbery gristle two or three inches thick. This thick skin protects it like a suit of armor. Harpoons cannot pierce the ocean sunfish's skin, and even the bullets from a Winchester rifle bounce harmlessly off it.

The safe, lazy life of the ocean sunfish does not call for much brain power, and that is fortunate. For this huge fish has a surprisingly small brain, just ½ inch long. In captivity, its lack of brains usually leads to a speedy death. If the ocean sunfish swims into a wall, it backs off and then stupidly slams into the wall again and again.

The ocean sunfish is not good to eat, for its flesh has a disagreeable odor. Fishermen do like to catch it, though. The oil from its fat liver makes a good grease on board ship. Fishermen also use the oil for treating sprains and bruises. But the few ocean sunfish that they catch are not enough to be a real threat to a fish that can lay 300 million eggs.

---

*10 or 11 feet = 3.0 or 3.3 meters*
*1 ton = 0.9 metric tons*
*14 feet = 4.3 meters*
*2¼ tons = 2.0 metric tons*
*¹⁄₂₀ inch = 1.27 millimeters*
*¹⁄₁₀ inch = 2.5 millimeters*
*½ inch = 1.27 centimeters*
*2 or 3 inches = 5.0 or 7.5 centimeters*

# The Longest Sleeper

## THE DORMOUSE

On a cold winter day, have you ever felt as though you'd like to crawl into bed and sleep until spring? Many animals do just that. In the fall, as the days grow shorter and a chill is in the air, they gather a store of food and retreat to a cozy den or burrow. There they go into a kind of deep sleep called hibernation. Some hibernators, like hamsters, sleep for a few days at a time, wake up to nibble a bit of food, and then go back to sleep again. Others sleep soundly right through the whole winter. Nature's champion sleepers are the dormice, who sleep for five or six months, from October to April. One dormouse, observed in England, slept for 6 months and 23 days straight.

The dormouse has a long, furry tail and looks more like a squirrel than a mouse. It lives like a squirrel, too. It scampers nimbly through the trees, feeding on nuts and seeds, and sometimes young shoots and bark. It is active mainly at night; it spends the day sleeping in its nest in a tree or in the ground. Curled up in a ball, with its tail wrapped around its head, the average dormouse is just as sound a sleeper as the Dormouse in *Alice in Wonderland*. Indeed, the "dor" part of its name comes from a French word, *dormir*, which means "to sleep." But deep as it is, the dormouse's daytime sleep is nothing compared to its winter hibernation.

In the early fall, the dormouse turns into an eating machine. It gobbles up every bit of food it can find and grows enormously fat. It is getting ready for its winter sleep. While it is hibernating, the dormouse will not eat. It will live on the supply of fat stored in its body. When it wakes in the spring, it may weigh only half as much as when it went to bed in the fall.

In October, the daytime sleeps of the dormouse grow longer and longer. Finally, it no longer wakes up at night, and it passes into a deeper sleep that is almost a coma. Its breathing slows down to only a few breaths a minute. Its heartbeat slows just as much. Its body temperature falls almost to the temperature of the air around it. Bright lights or loud noises would not disturb it. Even rolling a hibernating dormouse along a tabletop like a ball would not wake it. It sleeps on and on.

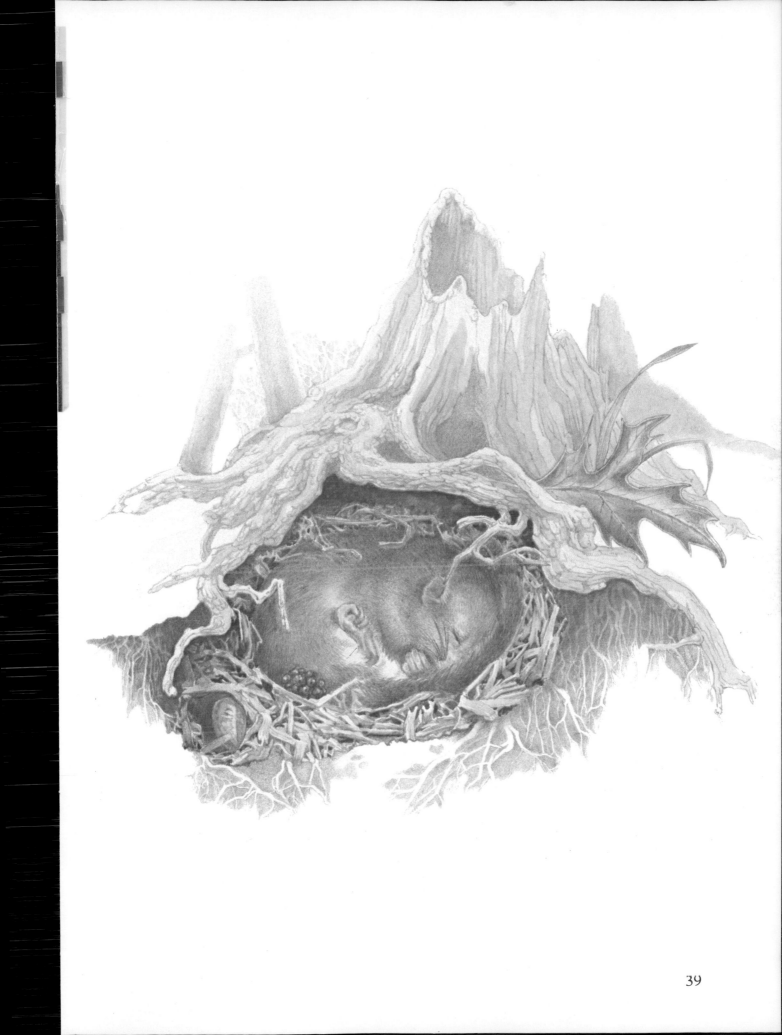

# The Largest Animal

## THE BLUE WHALE

Just imagine an animal bigger than the biggest dinosaur! The blue whale is the largest animal that ever lived on earth.

The biggest blue whale that was ever caught measured more than 109 feet from the tip of her jaw to the end of her tail. No one weighed her, but she may have weighed as much as 200 tons! (That is as much as about 20 African bush elephants or more than 2,000 men.) Even a newborn baby blue whale is bigger than most animals—about 25 feet long and weighing up to three tons. Growing to that size inside its mother's body in less than 11 months, it is the fastest-growing baby in the living world. After birth, drinking its mother's rich milk, it continues to grow at an astonishing rate of 200 pounds a day.

No land animal could ever grow as large as a whale. And in fact, if a whale is accidentally stranded on land, it is crushed under its own weight. The water of the ocean helps to hold up the enormous weight of a whale's body.

Whales look like fish, but they are not fish. They are mammals, just like cats and dogs and humans. Like other young mammals, a baby whale feeds on milk from its mother's body. And whales cannot breathe in the water as fish do. Though blue whales can stay underwater for about ten minutes at a time, they must then come up for a breath of air. A whale's nostrils form a "blowhole" on the top of its head. When the whale comes up to the surface and exhales, its moist breath forms a great spout above its head.

You might think that the world's largest animal would feed on other large animals—perhaps smaller whales or big fish. But the blue whale eats tiny shrimplike animals called krill. Each krill is only two inches long. The blue whale scoops them in in huge numbers—a ton of krill or more at one meal. Two sets of long, horny plates called whalebone or baleen hang down from the roof of the blue whale's mouth. The whale sucks in a huge mouthful of water, then strains out the krill on the baleen plates. During the year, the blue whales migrate through the world's oceans. They move from the cold seas near the North and South poles in the summer to warmer waters in the winter, following the schools of krill.

Unfortunately, these whales have been followed in turn by human whalers, who chase and kill them on huge factory ships. Once there were hundreds of thousands of blue whales in the world's oceans. But for many years whalers killed them faster than new blue whale babies could be born. Finally, there were fewer than a thousand left. Scientists warned that the blue whale might disappear from the earth forever. Now there are laws against killing blue whales, and their numbers are slowly increasing.

---

*109 feet = 33.0 meters*
*200 tons = 180.0 metric tons*
*25 feet = 7.6 meters*
*3 tons = 2.7 metric tons*
*200 pounds = 90.7 kilograms*
*2 inches = 5.0 centimeters*
*1 ton = 0.9 metric ton*

# The Largest Cactus
## THE SAGUARO

In the deserts of the southwestern United States, rows of towering green giants rise above the sandy ground. These are saguaros, the largest cactuses in the world. Some are 50 feet tall or more, and weigh as much as 12 tons. A skeleton of woody ribs inside the trunk and branches helps to support the giant cactus. Indeed, with its woody trunk and branches, the saguaro seems more like a tree than a juicy cactus.

The plants of the desert lead a strange life. Rain falls only twice a year, in the summer and winter. In the seasons between, the desert is dry. But cactuses and other desert plants can survive through the dry season because they store water in their plump stems. They do not lose water through their leaves as most plants do, for they have no leaves, only thin prickly thorns.

The saguaro is a champion water-storer. Its shallow roots spread over about 50 feet. When it rains, the roots soak up water from the sand—a single saguaro can take in as much as a ton of water after just one rainfall. The water is stored in a grooved channel in the stem, which expands like an accordion. (Sometimes saguaros take in so much water that they explode!)

The summer rain in the desert brings a burst of flowers. Each of the saguaro's cream-colored flowers lasts only one day, opening at night and wilting by the next afternoon. But there are so many buds that the saguaro continues to bloom for several weeks. When the flowers die, the fruits begin to grow. As they ripen, the fruits split open to show crimson pulp with thousands of tiny black seeds. Mice and ants run up the stems to gather the seeds, and white-winged doves feed on them, too. But some seeds fall to the ground and sprout.

The seed of the giant saguaro is no bigger than a pinhead. During its early years, no one would ever guess that it was going to grow into a giant. It takes two years for a seedling to grow just ¼ inch high. Even after thirty years, it is scarcely 3 feet tall. The first branches do not appear until the saguaro has lived for 60 or 70 years—a whole lifetime for a human. The giant cactus can live and grow for 200 years. Holes in its trunk provide shelter for many animals, from woodpeckers and elf owls and mice to snakes, lizards, spiders, and moths.

Saguaros used to be plentiful in the West. For hundreds of years, Indians used their woody skeletons as frameworks for their shelters and made jam from their fruits; and still the plants thrived. But when white settlers came to the West, they brought many changes that made life difficult for the giant cactuses. The settlers' cattle trampled the young seedlings and the desert bushes whose shade the young plants need to grow. Ranchers killed off the coyotes and mountain lions that used to eat small animals, so the mice and other seed-eaters multiplied. Today most of the saguaros that remain are protected in the Saguaro National Monument. But few young seedlings can be found, and some are stolen by people to sell in plant stores. When today's giants of the West die, there may be no more saguaros to replace them.

---

*50 feet = 15.2 meters*
*12 tons = 10.8 metric tons*
*1 ton = 0.9 metric ton*
*¼ inch = 6.3 millimeters*
*3 feet = 91.4 centimeters*

# The Biggest Eater

## THE SHREW

What was the biggest meal you ever ate? Can you imagine eating an amount of food equal to your whole weight at a single meal? That is what nature's champion eaters, the shrews, can do. One shrew was observed eating 3¼ ounces of food in just eight days. That does not sound like very much. But the shrew itself weighed only ⅛ ounce, less than the weight of a single copper penny!

The shrew lives a short but busy life. Its inner clock seems to be speeded up. It goes through a miniature "day" every three hours. During this time it feeds and snatches short, restless naps. If a shrew is forced to go without food for two or three hours, it will die.

During its active periods, a shrew is constantly on the move, scurrying about the ground and through underground tunnels, looking for food. It sniffs about with its long, sensitive snout, and gobbles down all the insects it can find. Snails and worms and any other creatures small enough for a shrew to overpower may be its prey. It will even attack a mouse twice its size if one happens to come into its burrow. (On the open ground, a mouse moves too quickly for a shrew to catch.) Nuts, berries, seeds, and the bodies of dead animals help to round out the diet for the ever-hungry shrew.

A shrew looks like a tiny, helpless creature. Smaller than a mouse, with soft brownish fur,

the shrew has small eyes and no ears at all on the outside of its head. It makes up for its poor eyesight with its sensitive nose. Its hearing is good, too. In fact, scientists think that the shrew may use its high-pitched squeaks for echo-location to help it find its prey, as bats do. Musk glands on the shrew's sides produce a strong, unpleasant odor, which helps to discourage many enemies. If an enemy attacks, the shrew becomes a tiny ball of fury. It is ready to turn its sharp, slashing teeth on anyone or anything—from another shrew to a human handling it. Shrews are often so bad-tempered, in fact, that a quarrelsome person is sometimes called a "shrew."

The female shrew leads a busier life than the male. In a year, she may raise three litters of four to ten young each. Newborn shrews weigh only $\frac{1}{100}$ ounce. But they grow quickly in their cozy, grass-lined nest. Before they are a month old, they are ready to be on their own. They will live at just as fast a pace as their mother. At 15 months—if they survive that long—they will already be old.

Shrews are very common in many parts of the world. They are seldom seen, as they scurry about under the grass cover or leaf litter. But these champion eaters are a big help to farmers in their fight against pests.

$3\frac{1}{4}$ ounces = 92.1 grams
$\frac{1}{8}$ ounce = 3.5 grams
$\frac{1}{100}$ ounce = 0.28 grams

# The Largest Snake

## THE ANACONDA

Most people have strong feelings about snakes—they either love them or hate them. Some people have worshipped them as gods, while others have feared them as agents of the Devil. Today people still have a lot of wrong ideas about snakes. Even the "facts" are not always certain.

How large is the largest snake, for example? There have been stories of snakes more than 100 feet long. But most experts believe that the largest snake ever measured was an anaconda, shot by a geologist in Colombia. Using a steel tape measure, he measured the snake's length as 37½ feet and estimated its weight at about 1,000 pounds. When he went back later to skin the snake, though, it was gone! Apparently it was only stunned by the bullets and recovered and slithered away. Some people say this story can't be true. Most anacondas are no more than about 20 feet. And although the New York Zoological Society many years ago offered a prize of $5,000 for an anaconda more than 30 feet long, the prize has never been claimed.

Anacondas are heavy snakes. A large adult is as thick around as a man's waist. It is extremely strong. Anacondas belong to the boa family. Like other constrictors, they catch their prey by wrapping several coils about its body and squeezing. They do not crush it or break its bones. Instead, the snake merely tightens its grip around the victim's chest so that it cannot expand, and the animal suffocates.

Anacondas spend much of their time in the water—in rivers and swamps of tropical South America. (Another name for the snake is the water boa.) They are usually active at night. During the day they lie hidden or stretch out on a low tree branch to sunbathe. Often the anaconda lies silently by a river bank, waiting for an animal to come down to drink. Then it strikes, dragging its prey down into the water. Small deer, wild pigs called peccaries, and large rodents are meals for anacondas. The big snakes also eat young crocodiles and turtles, as well as fish. Like other snakes, the anaconda can open its jaws amazingly wide to swallow animals far larger than its head. After a particularly big meal, such as a peccary, the snake may not need to feed again for several months.

Like most snakes, the anaconda bites to defend itself. The wounds are deep but not poisonous, and they heal quickly.

Anacondas give birth to live young. A mother can have 20 to 40 or even more young each year. The little ones are miniature copies of their parents, each two or three feet long. It will take years for them to grow up into giants. Since anacondas never stop growing, a real oldtimer of 20 years or so might indeed grow to be more than 35 feet long.

---

*100 feet = 30.5 meters*
*37½ feet = 11.4 meters*
*1,000 pounds = 453.6 kilograms*
*20 feet = 6.1 meters*
*30 feet = 9.1 meters*
*2 or 3 feet = 61.0 or 91.4 centimeters*
*35 feet = 10.6 meters*

# The Most Poisonous

## THE BLACK WIDOW SPIDER

Do creepy, crawly spiders make you shudder? Many people are afraid of them. Usually, though, there's no reason to fear spiders. Most are shy creatures that would rather run away and hide than bite. Even if they do bite, they seldom cause more discomfort than a bee sting. But at least one kind of spider deserves to be treated with the greatest caution—the black widow, the most poisonous spider in the world. Weight for weight, the black widow's venom is 15 times stronger than that of the prairie rattlesnake. Though the spider injects a much smaller amount of venom than a snake does, its bite can kill a human being. The spider venom is a nerve poison that can cause great pain and paralyze the body.

The black widow spider is found throughout the United States (particularly in the southern states) and in Mexico. It lives in cool, dark places—in cellars and sheds, under porches, and in piles of rubbish. In rural homes with outdoor privies, the underside of a toilet seat is a favorite place for the black widow to hide. (Often its bite is not only dangerous, but also embarrassing!) Like other spiders, the black widow does not usually bite unless it thinks it is being attacked.

The female black widow spider is the dangerous one. She is easy to recognize by her shiny, velvety black body, about ½ inch long, and the red hour-glass marking on the underside of her belly. The male black widow spider is much smaller, about ⅙ inch long. He does not have enough venom to be harmful to a person.

Like other spiders, the black widow spins a web of silk that is made in special glands inside its body. The web is a thick crisscross of threads. On one side there is a short funnel of silk, which serves as a shelter for the spider while it is waiting for its prey. The spider sits on its web, with its feet touching the strands. If an insect flies into the web, the spider feels the vibrations. It dashes out along the silken threads (it knows which ones are not sticky) and quickly wraps up its victim in a blanket of silk. Then it paralyzes the insect with a bite from its poison fangs. The spider injects a special digesting juice, which softens the victim's body so the spider can easily "drink" it up.

The male black widow spider makes a web and eats insects only when he is young. He can survive for the rest of his life on stored-up energy from his early meals. The female, however, continues to eat during her whole lifetime.

The black widow spider gets its name from its color and from the belief that the female eats her mate as soon as she has mated with him. But she may not be as deadly a mate as she seems. A male can mate with a number of female black widow spiders. Each time, he prepares for the mating by spinning a little web and placing on it a drop of liquid containing his sperm. Then he picks up the drop with two special "legs" and places it in the body of his mate. That's hard work for a spider, and each time he grows weaker. His last mate kills him and eats him and becomes the true "black widow."

---

*½ inch = 1.3 centimeters*
*⅙ inch = 4.2 millimeters*

# The Longest Jumper

## THE KANGAROO

Nature's champion jumpers are the kangaroos, which live in Australia. A kangaroo is really built for leaping. About the size of a tall man, it stands upright on long, heavy hind legs and balances itself with a long, thick tail. A kangaroo can easily outjump a person. As it bounds along, it often makes jumps of 25 feet or more. The longest kangaroo jump ever recorded was about 42 feet—about six times the kangaroo's height. Kangaroos are good high jumpers, too. One kangaroo, being chased by dogs, cleared a wood pile 10½ feet high with ease. (Only the best human jumpers can leap even 7 feet high.) Kangaroos are awkward when they are moving slowly on four legs, but they can bound along swiftly on their big hind legs, reaching speeds of up to 35 miles an hour. In 1927, in Sydney, Australia, a kangaroo and a racehorse were put in a race, and the kangaroo won easily.

At home in the wild, kangaroos use their speed to escape from enemies such as the dingo, a wild dog. They travel about over the countryside in groups called mobs. Usually a mob of kangaroos includes one large male, his mates, and a number of younger males and females. The leader of the mob defends himself against other male kangaroos by boxing with his front paws. Sometimes tame kangaroos are taught to box with human fighters, to the delight of Australian sports fans.

Like nearly all the mammals in Australia, kangaroos are marsupials. A female marsupial raises her young in a pouch in her belly.

A baby kangaroo, or joey, is less than an inch long when it is born, and it is naked and blind. Somehow it climbs up its mother's belly and into her pouch. There it promptly clamps onto one of the nipples inside and begins to drink its mother's milk. The joey stays inside its mother's pouch, drinking milk and growing. After a time it begins to go out every now and then, and nibbles on the tender grass. When the joey is about eight months old, it leaves its 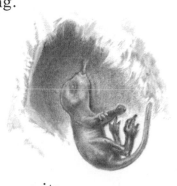 mother's pouch for good. But it still stays with her for several years more.

Kangaroos roam around, feeding on grass and other green plants. Their sharp teeth cut the grass off very close to the ground, and this can ruin pasture land for sheep and cattle. Kangaroos also drink more than their share at water holes, although they can go without water for a long time if they have to. Even a nine-foot fence can't keep the leaping kangaroos out of pastures and farmlands. To Australian sheep raisers and farmers, kangaroos are not champions, but pests.

---

*25 feet = 7.6 meters*
*42 feet = 12.8 meters*
*10½ feet = 3.2 meters*
*7 feet = 2.1 meters*
*35 miles = 56.3 kilometers*
*1 inch = 2.54 centimeters*
*9 feet = 2.7 meters*

# The Best Jumper

## THE FLEA

Kangaroos make the longest jumps of any animal in the world—but are they really nature's champion jumpers? Some people think the tiny flea has a better claim to the title. A flea can leap 8 inches high and cover a distance of 13 inches in a single jump. That doesn't sound like very much, compared with a kangaroo. But most fleas are less than ¼ inch long. They can jump more than 100 times their body length! (A kangaroo can jump only six times its body length.) And fleas are the most tireless jumpers in the world. Scientists have watched rat fleas jump steadily for three days straight, 600 times an hour, without stopping.

For years scientists wondered how fleas could possibly jump so well. Even the fastest possible muscle contractions could not move their little legs fast enough. Finally it was discovered that part of the flea's body, near the tops of its strong back legs, contains a rubbery elastic material that scientists call resilin.

When a flea is getting ready to jump, it crouches down and squeezes its resilin together. When this super-rubber snaps back, the flea goes flying through the air.

Fleas live on the skin of animals and suck their blood. Their bites are irritating, and can spread disease. The flea often has to make a quick escape when the animal it is biting tries to scratch or pick it off. Its ability to quickly hop away helps save its life.

A mother flea usually leaves her animal host to lay her eggs. She places them in a pile of trash, or under a carpet, or in some other place where her young will find food and safety. The eggs hatch into tiny wormlike maggots, which feed on dust and dirt or tiny scraps of food dropped by humans or other animals. Then each maggot spins a silken cocoon and changes into an adult. It comes out of the cocoon ready to hop onto a passing animal.

Flea circuses used to be a favorite attraction at fairs. The flea trainer usually used fleas that live on humans, and fed them on his own arm. Fleas are really not smart enough to learn to do tricks, although the trainer said they could. It was really the trainer's trick. He harnessed his fleas with fine silk threads or gold or silver wires and then attached the ends to tiny rings, carts, and other props. Working with a magnifying glass, the trainer would guide the fleas on their harnesses so that their natural movements made them seem to jump through hoops, juggle, walk a tightrope, and pull objects several times their own weight. A flea circus, complete with routines such as chariot races and sword fights, was a fascinating sight.

---

*8 inches = 20.3 centimeters*
*13 inches = 33.0 centimeters*
*¼ inch = 6.3 millimeters*

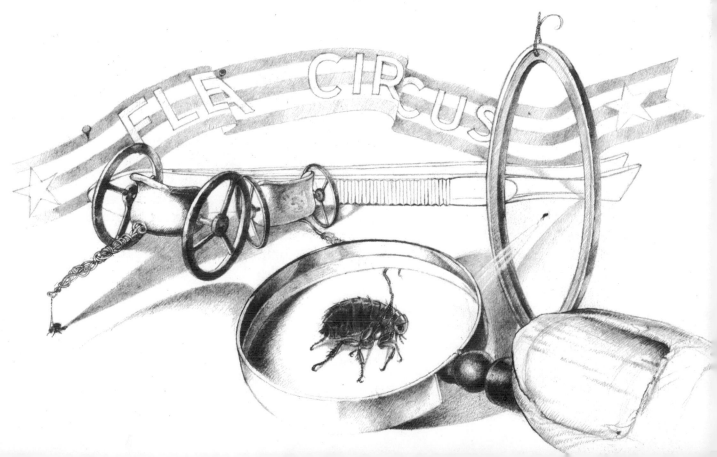

# The Fastest Swimmer

## THE SAILFISH

One of the biggest thrills of fishing is to hook a sailfish. The fish leaps and dives, fighting with tremendous strength. Each time it breaks the surface of the water, with a shower of foam, it raises the great fin on its back, like the sail of a boat. It darts and dives so quickly, disappearing under the water and reappearing in another place, that it seems there must surely be two fish, or more.

Over short distances, the sailfish is the fastest swimmer. No one is sure exactly how fast this fish can really swim. But in one series of tests with a stopwatch, a sailfish took out 100 feet of fishing line in just three seconds. That works out to more than 68 miles an hour. (The cheetah, the fastest land animal, can reach a speed of about 70 miles an hour in short sprints.)

The sailfish is built for speed. It is a big fish, up to 20 feet long and weighing as much as 1,000 pounds. Its upper jaw is a long, swordlike beak. Its long, cigar-shaped body is a marvel of streamlining. When it is swimming at top speed, it folds its fins close to its body so that it can slip smoothly through the water. The huge "sail" folds neatly into a groove on the upper part of the sailfish's body. The powerful tail lashes back and forth to send the sailfish streaking through the water.

At the end of a burst of speed, the sailfish raises its sail to keep its body from rolling over. It also raises the sail when it is sunning itself at the surface of the water. It may use the sail to catch the winds and skim along like a sailboat. When a school of sailfish swim together, they look like a fleet of boats.

The sailfish is a relative of the

swordfish, which was named for its long, flat "sword." But the sword of a sailfish is rounded, not flat. It uses this long beak to catch its prey. It swims around a school of mackerel or other small fish with its sail partly raised, herding them together. Then it swims into the school, lashing its head from side to side, beating the small fish with its beak. Many of the small fish are killed or stunned. Then the sailfish slowly swims about, snapping up the small fish as they sink.

Sailfish are such exciting game fish that the sportsmen are very concerned about protecting them from dying out. Although they are good to eat, most of the sailfish that are hooked today are not pulled on board. The people who catch them just pull them over to the side of the boat and fasten a tag to one fin. Then they remove the hook and let the sailfish go. Scientists are using reports of tagged sailfish to gather information on the habits of this champion swimmer.

---

*100 feet = 30.5 meters*
*70 miles = 112.6 kilometers*
*68 miles = 109.4 kilometers*
*20 feet = 6.1 meters*
*1,000 pounds = 453.6 kilograms*

# The Keenest Sense of Smell

## THE SILKWORM MOTH

The animal with the keenest sense of smell does not have a nose. It is a moth—the silkworm moth. It "smells" scents with two feathery antennae, or feelers, attached to the top of its head.

A moth starts its life as a tiny egg, laid on a twig or in some other protected place. The creature that hatches from the egg does not look like a moth at all. It is a caterpillar, and its main occupation is eating. It chews up leaves at an enormous rate and grows so fat that its outer covering becomes too tight. Several times it must shed its "skin" in order to continue to eat and grow. At last it is ready for an amazing change. With silk thread formed in special glands in its body, it spins a cocoon around itself. A silkworm's cocoon is made up of a single thread of silk, about 1,000 yards long.

Shut up inside the cocoon, the caterpillar begins to change. At times it almost seems to melt and flow. Gradually a new shape takes form. Short, stubby caterpillar legs disappear, and six long insect legs appear. Larger eyes and new feath-ery antennae develop on the head. Two pairs of wings, neatly folded, grow out on the creature's back. It is turning into a moth! When the change is complete, the moth cuts its way out of the cocoon.

As a caterpillar, the insect spent all its time eating. Now, as an adult moth, it has a different goal in life: to find another moth of the opposite sex, and to mate. Yet the closest possible mate may be miles away. How can they find each other? The female moth produces a special scent, which is carried by the winds. Thousands of sense cells in the male's antennae are tuned to pick up exactly that scent. When he finds

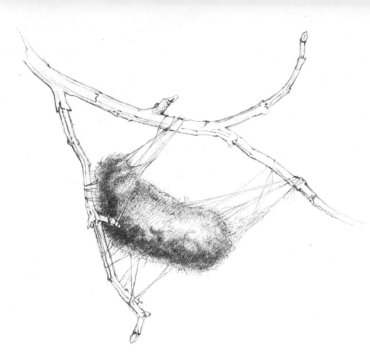

it, he flutters up excitedly and flies upwind until he reaches the female.

In one experiment, scientists released male silkworm moths from a train moving away from the laboratory where the female silkworm moths were kept. They found that the male moths could still pick up the scent of the females at an amazing distance of nearly seven miles!

Modern silkworm moths do not need to use their amazing sense of smell. Their matings are carefully arranged for them. Silkworms are true domestic animals. They have been bred by humans for thousands of years—so long that there are no longer any wild ones left. The domestic silkworms probably could not survive without humans to keep them warm and protected and feed them the mulberry leaves on which they thrive.

---

*1,000 yards = 914.4 meters*
*7 miles = 11.2 kilometers*

# The Largest Nest

## THE BALD EAGLE

Birds' nests come in all sizes and shapes—from hanging baskets, to platforms of twigs held together by mud, to holes in tree trunks. Nature's champion nest builders are the bald eagles, the national bird of the United States. Their nests may not be the prettiest, but they are surely the largest.

Bald eagles mate for life, and they are faithful not only to their mates, but to their nests as well. They build a nest out of a pile of sticks, some of them as much as six feet long. The nest is lined with weeds and earth. At first the nest is about two feet deep. But as the eagles sit on their eggs and raise the little eaglets, they gradually trample the nest flat. So the next year, when they return to raise a new brood, they build a new layer. One bald eagle nest, near Vermilion, Ohio, was used every year for 35 years. (Perhaps the children of the original pair of eagles carried on after they died.) This enormous nest was built in the fork of a hickory tree, more than 80 feet above the ground. By the time the nest finally came crashing down in a storm, it measured 8½ feet across, 12 feet deep, and weighed about 2 tons! Another nest, in Florida, was 20 feet deep.

A bald eagle is not really bald at all. It gets its name from the white feathers that grow on its head. These feathers make it look bald from a distance, because its body and wings are covered with dark brown feathers.

The bald eagle was chosen as the national bird of the United States in 1782, because it looked like such a proud bird. But Benjamin Franklin objected. He wanted the wild turkey to be chosen instead, and claimed that the bald eagle is "a bird of bad moral character who does not get his living honestly." Perhaps there was some truth to Franklin's arguments. The bald eagle often feeds on the bodies of animals that have died or been killed by other animals. And sometimes a bald eagle will swoop down to attack an osprey that has caught a fish, snatching the osprey's catch away from it. But bald eagles do catch their own prey, too. They can dive into a lake to snatch up a fish, swoop down to catch a hopping rabbit, or overtake a duck on the wing. Even their habit of eating dead animals plays a part in the world of nature: they help to clean up the landscape and "recycle" the materials of life.

Today the bald eagle is in danger. Many farmers and ranchers complain that eagles steal their livestock, and they often shoot the big birds. The use of DDT and other pesticides has made many bald eagles unable to have young. Others can still lay eggs, but the shells may be so thin that they crack before the chicks can hatch. And as people build roads and houses over more of the land, there is less and less room for bald eagles to build their nests. Unless something is done soon, America's national bird may disappear from its native land.

_____

*6 feet = 1.8 meters*
*2 feet = 60.9 centimeters*
*80 feet = 24.3 meters*
*8½ feet = 2.6 meters*
*12 feet = 3.6 meters*
*2 tons = 1.8 metric tons*
*20 feet = 6.1 meters*

# The Largest Fish

## THE WHALE SHARK

"Shark!" That cry is usually enough to frighten the bravest swimmer. Sharks have a well-earned reputation as vicious killers who can tear a person apart with their slashing teeth. But the largest shark of all—the whale shark—is a gentle giant. It is so even-tempered that a swimmer can swim around it and even climb on its back, without fear of a bite or a slap from the whale shark's huge tail.

The largest whale shark ever reliably measured was certainly as big as some of the whales for which it is named. It was 59 feet long, and its weight was estimated at close to 90,000 pounds. Some whalers, used to estimating the size of sperm whales, have reported sighting whale sharks more than 70 feet long.

Even whale shark babies are champion-sized. They hatch from eggs a foot long or more, larger than those of any other living animal.

Whale sharks can dive to great depths in the ocean. But they spend most of their time swimming lazily in the surface waters. They feed on schools of tiny fish, such as sardines and anchovies, and on squids, shrimps, crabs, and other small ocean creatures. Like the big whales, the whale shark strains its food out of the water. The water it gulps into its mouth passes over rows of strainers in its gills, called gill rakers. They look very much like miniature whalebones. The whale shark does not have huge, slashing teeth like the man-eating sharks. Instead, it has about 3,000 tiny teeth, each only ⅛ inch long, arranged in about 300 rows in its jaws. No one knows how the whale shark uses all these teeth. Scientists do know that it does not chew with them, for it swallows its food whole.

The whale shark's spotted skin is the thickest skin of any living animal. The skin of a 60-foot-long whale shark is nine inches thick! A harpoon can barely penetrate into this tough skin. And if it is harpooned, the whale shark can tighten the muscles in its skin and turn it into a sheet of living armor. Other harpoons just bounce off it harmlessly, often bent as though they had hit a solid steel wall.

As the whale shark swims, it makes a sort of croaking sound. Scientists think that it may use the sound for echo-location to find its way around, as the whales and dolphins do.

Whale sharks present no danger to humans except by accident—they may bump into a small boat and overturn it. Indeed, these huge fish seem to enjoy rubbing against boats, and may keep it up for an hour. Perhaps they find the boats ideal scratching posts for getting rid of parasites, unwelcome creatures that cling to their skin.

---

*59 feet = 17.9 meters*
*90,000 pounds = 40,824 kilograms*
*70 feet = 21.3 meters*
*⅛ inch = 3.2 millimeters*
*60 feet = 18.2 meters*
*9 inches = 22.8 centimeters*

# The Loudest Insect

## THE CICADA

On hot summer days, the quiet of the countryside is often broken by a deafening noise. It sounds like a scissors grinder, or perhaps a train whistle. Sometimes the noise is so loud that two people cannot even hear each other if they try to have a conversation. This noise is made by crowds of insects called cicadas—champion noisemakers.

These insects begin their life when a female cicada drills a small hole in a twig and deposits her tiny eggs there. She lays so many eggs in the twig that the tree or shrub may be badly damaged. The young cicada that hatches from each egg does not look like its mother. It has no wings, and its front legs are broad and strong, good for digging. It is called a nymph at this stage of its life. It wriggles out of the hole in the twig, drops to the ground, and quickly burrows down into the soil. It will spend most of its life in the soil, sucking the juices from the roots of plants.

Some cicadas take two years to grow up; others are not full grown until they are 17 years old. But finally the nymph changes into an adult. It crawls up out of the ground

and onto a tree where it sheds its old skin. Now its new form is uncovered. It has four thin wings that it folds over its body like a roof when the insect is not flying. The cicada will live no more than a few weeks longer. This is the most dangerous time of its life. Birds may swoop down and gobble it up. A wasp called the cicada killer may sting the cicada and carry it home as food for its young. But if the cicada is lucky, it will live long enough to mate.

In order to mate, a male cicada must find a female cicada of just the right kind. Cicadas find their mates by singing. In most species only the males sing. Each kind of cicada has its own special song, different from the sounds of other species. Some cicadas sing so loudly that they can be heard ¼ mile away. The male cicadas have two sound chambers in their abdomens. Each is covered by a membrane called a tymbal that the male can pop in and out like the lid of a tin can. The male can make his tymbals vibrate very fast—from 100 to nearly 500 times a second. These vibrations make the sound of his song.

As the cicada sings, other cicadas hear his song and fly to meet him. Soon there is a crowd of cicadas, both males and females, perched on the tree branches. Birds zero in on the sound and swoop down to catch a meal. But many of the insects mate and start a new generation of cicadas on its way.

_____

*¼ mile = 0.4 kilometer*

# The Oldest Living Thing

## THE BRISTLECONE PINE

The oldest living things on earth are not people or elephants or even the long-lived giant tortoises. They are trees—bristlecone pines. Many bristlecone pines living today in Nevada, California, and Utah were already old at the time of the Roman Empire, 2,000 years ago. The oldest of all the living bristlecone pines, up on the White Mountains in California, is more than 4,600 years old! It is named Methuselah, after the famous Bible character who is said to have lived for 969 years—longer than any other person.

How can anyone know for sure how old a tree is—especially a tree as old as a bristlecone pine? As a tree grows, its trunk gets wider, as a new ring of wood is formed. Growth rings show up clearly on the cut surface of a tree trunk. (Each ring represents a year's growth.) Scientists can study the growth rings of a living tree without harming the tree by cutting out a thin core of wood, about the size of a pencil. A bristlecone pine's growth rings are much narrower than those of most trees, so narrow that a microscope must be used to count them. The tree grows very slowly, adding perhaps only an inch of width in 100 years. Even the oldest trees are only about 30 feet tall and perhaps 12 feet across the trunk.

Bristlecone pines **look** old. Their trunks and branches are bent and twisted. Grains of sand and ice crystals whipped by the winds on the high mountain slopes have scoured them nearly bare. In trees more than 1,500 years old, usually only a thin strip of living bark remains, running up the protected side of the trunk, away from the windy blasts. Water and food materials for the tree are carried along this strip of bark. The rest of the wood is dead, but sticky resin protects it from drying out or decaying. Some of the branches are bare; others are crowned with "bottlebrushes" of short green needles. The great roots may be partly bare, exposed over hundreds and thousands of years as the rocky soil was washed or blown away.

Not all bristlecone pines grow to such a great age. The trees living at lower altitudes, where there is plenty of soil and water and shelter from the wind, grow quickly and soon die and decay. The real champion ancients live high up on the rocky mountain slopes. Their life is a hard one, but the longest of all.

---

*1 inch = 2.54 centimeters*
*30 feet = 9.1 meters*
*12 feet = 3.6 meters*

# The Smartest

## THE HUMAN BEING

There is one animal that might be called the champion of champions. It can fly higher than an Alpine chough, faster than a spine-tailed swift, and farther than an arctic tern. It could win a race with a cheetah on land, and with a sailfish in the water. It builds houses far larger than the nest of a bald eagle and ships bigger than the body of a blue whale. It can hear sounds that even a bat could not hear and generate more electricity than an electric eel. It is stronger than an elephant, more deadly than a black widow spider. This champion of champions is a human being.

We humans could not accomplish all these things alone. Our bodies are weak compared with those of some other animals, and our eyes, ears, and other senses are not the keenest. The secret of our achievements is a three-pound, wrinkled, jellylike structure inside our bony skulls: the human brain. Humans have the most highly developed intelligence of all the animals on our planet. Using our amazing brain, we have been able to build tools and machines to extend the reach of our senses and our strength. We can imagine things that have never existed, and then build them to the shape of our dreams. We can share our dreams with others and work toward future goals. We have become masters of our planet, controlling the lives of other species and changing the face of the world.

Today we stand at a crossroads. We hold the power to make the world a better place for all its creatures—or to destroy all life. We are the most intelligent of all creatures. Will we be wise enough to make a success of our role as caretaker of life on earth?

VOLTAIRE

EINSTEIN

MOZART

SHAKESPEARE

BOOKER T. WASHINGTON

MARIE
CURIE

LEONARDO
DA VINCI

ARISTOTLE

PHARAOH AKHNATON

# Index

(References to pictures are in *italic type*.)

## About the Authors

Dr. Alvin Silverstein is a professor and head of the biology department at the College of Staten Island of CUNY. Virginia B. Silverstein is a translator of Russian scientific literature. Together the Silversteins have produced six children, three novels, and more than fifty published children's books. The Silverstein clan lives in a big, old house in Lebanon, New Jersey.

## About the Illustrator

Art is everywhere in the life of Jean Zallinger. Not only is she the illustrator of about 60 books, including four award winners, but she is an associate professor at the Paier School of Art in Hamden, Connecticut; she is married to painter Rudolph Zallinger; her son Peter is an illustrator; and one of her daughters, Kristina, is a painter and graphic artist. Mr. and Mrs. Zallinger live in North Haven, Connecticut.